Porcupine

To Cherrie,

Hope you like it,
honestly there's not
much to get.

Porcupine

Jack Cunnington

BEARDED BADGER
PUBLISHING CO.

Contents

no peachy prayers

the world i have seen
this night is
turning itself to
stone and so i have made
an igneous little rock out of love
and i am paddling my
way over the edge
of tomorrow.

no trendy réchauffé

a friend is a slippery thing,
you can try to be one,
an idling wriggler in the membranes
of thought-feeling.

or try to be,
an enemy
and more like
a nail between ribs
or tooth-picks
under toe-nails
a shuddering feeling
with two names
and a handkerchief.

be the wriggling,
gyrating disturbance
but with love.
hated with smiles
all embarrassments
and forced chuckles.
but that's love really
isn't it?

wind yourself
up like a yo-yo
or the naval captain
run low on bovril and
never eat sleep or
dream. and when
you're forced to eat
toast in the afternoon
out of pity

know then
that you are loved
eternally.

Landings

I have found myself very familiar with my window frames,
and my sills and the lights on my landing.
I have been learning to climb along the walls,
and make my rooms new and free.
my garden is becoming new again
and for grace and lack of spring
I see a bloom of the dead.
the thing grows its arms which become tendrils that touch my
face softly;
they only ask that I watch them like children.

at the bottom of the garden I see a rupturing mole's hill,
where he moves up and down clawing at the sod,
the starred nose of an old thing; blind and swimming,
etching bas-reliefs into the caves beneath me.

I see his head move,
how strange it is
to be seeming
to be breathing
in tandem with a dying world.

The last will and testament of Thomas Baltby
(For Sam)

here, on and yet beside my death-bed,
I bequeath unto thee, my dearest john:
my drivers license, one hundred and
forty-two penny black stamps (stapled
into 1.42 one-pound bundles), smoke matches
acquired from a country i have since forgotten.
it did have a demilitarised zone, mind.

a fish that walks and a dog that talks,
my prized collection of those VHS tape covers
made to look like leather-bound books,
that one Durer you & I were always fond of,
pete the prisoner's fishing rod, stained with
the morose thrill of a japanese water garden.

there's gunner's gun, strap's strap, four
teeth from the hydra, thunderbird one, a
rusted air rifle, £10 left in a drawer, potions
of rice and rum, 3 tuffys and a VCR to read
with. don't do anything dodgy with that
license will you?

variations on a shadow

since he had died
i had missed a certain
lingering fear of shadows,
where before I once cowered
over an excess of bubbles
and a saucepan, scared to score
the back of my own hand like pig fat.
I wished I could drink his bile and
understand him in rages as he scored
the small of my back. like pig fat.
I tried to understand him removing
himself in front of me, so devoid of
his own shame that i would feel it for him.
at times a face or two that grew
indistinguishable from itself, as each
other. both separate screaming beasts as
people, giving birth to one another
endlessly. without loss or any knowledge
of itself or without declaring itself the same.
how does one tell? one, cocks removed into the
glaring phosphorescence of spitting, snarling
tube-light. another pulled out and into a milk bottle
and more and more there I am. the third, crawling
out and back into itself. the shadow gladly recedes.
I miss that self-same trace of smoke that chokes
unknowing younger lungs and rhymes childishly
with itself. now only a noticed space on an empty 'a'.
the antifreeze drink you poured, the drink you barely
touch. I am as scared of you as you are of him.
half the man hates the self. where does that leave
the rest of us? Why are we both not so content
with being as miserable as limping smoke? like a rat
ruptured to blood in the bushes beside the canal.

you can't watch that. you and me both.
we don't weep because we can't and that is how I
sleep at night. I rest my head on your death-march.
the shadow snarls like tube-light and sneers to bring
me half-frozen supper from where it finds its own.
All I could do was take from you. take in fear
of what i hadn't had. smoke and
shadow retreat into tube-light
he had gone, yet
the two had
merged into
one.

the gentler-man

the gentler-man leaves
hand-written notes on
bed-side tables for beloved
daughters/mothers/husbands
or sister's lovers.

the gentler-man kneels
pewside/ringside/courtside
or infanticide. gleeful cheers;
pocket money for all!

the gentler-man experiences
himself backwards through
time. thinks himself a child
more by the day.

the gentler-man expresses
great admiration for all the
rocks: picnic at hanging;
suicide at egg. so on
and so forth.

the gentler-man reinvents
himself his own belief in
the morning. so that he may,
at the going down of sun,
remember them.

the gentler-man is always at
once ferociously attacked in an
elevator, and in print by
Ryszard Kapuściński.

the gentler-man is a dog left
in a hot car who has decided
not to pant. he has made his
peace with this.

the gentler-man has a heartbeat
like a double-bass and he limps
like a piano. he was attacked in
asda. that was jazz.

the gentler-man has read marx,
he knows of Eliot's leading-man
appeal and that inside of a
dog, it is too dark to read.

the gentler-man knows
where he ends and
I begin. I have made my
peace with that.

the gentler-man hopes that
he can take my children
and wife away. in many ways,
they have already left.

the gentler-man has left his front
door open and gone into the
garden. you could do that
back then.

the gentler-man has begun a career
in plagiarism in pencil, lies in pen,
and counts the time with Tiny Tim in
quarter-tones to ten.

the gentler-man plays the spoons
in the anderson shelter. mother and
I began to cry and relive our youths
spent on peckham rye.

The Florist, or The Love-Song of Albert Fish

I have decided to begin leaving flowers
in the ground. I can no longer look them
in the eye and unseam the backs of leaves,
pausing horribly to inhale erotic dreams of
chlorophyll.

I have watched the garden-men making evil love
in the rose bush, fondling pollen onto their
nose-tips and thrusting unmentionably into
one-another's vision of waspish ecstasy.

I shall never again undress the graceful bud
of the rose. I resign myself to the thorn;
rubbed into my tender gums, stoking fires
with the cruel covetous hooks of my garden.
I die to busy myself; flowers are just bones
for the dying.

behind the coves are the moors

yards and gardens lose me still; we disappoint them.
traced like they are through lilting silt and piling mud,
singing hills and frightened song
our places marked in steps along...

stepping more on reeds than rocks the toes caress and slowly slip.
boy's heels move down like a mussel's grip.
crabbing boys; grandad plays
by the brown sands it sees in the days.

only young; the kite so gripp'd,
off the point where boats are slipped.
and gracing the burning finger folds;
the rope moves the skin from itself.
a boy.
so young.
himself a rose.
briars for family.
Auntie took us aboard the train.

all the way our hands were tied: abiding by the countryside
And sleeping over on the hill
Where shepherds hark and farmers till
the train it chuffs along its way
carrying the boys from Saturday
hens and cocks and clouds descend
To make the evening time a friend.
dressed in warmer clothes it still:
flutters to the heavens.

Suicide, or Play-Doh Sunrise

The end of life had passed me by,
Whilst I dreamt of play-doh sunrise,
Out of the house and past the gate,
I'd never left the house so late!

I could never leave. So I slumped
sobbing to the porch. I traced a chalk
outline to save him the trouble and shot
myself twice in the head.

He'll happen upon me with such
startled eyes that
He'll wordlessly dream that he'd seen
a play-doh sunrise.

Bee's Town

I

As I lay dying, I could not help myself but
to stare at the brutish smoke-stack boys
breaking the delicate bones in the arms of
tree branches. I, a gentle, screaming joy
to the drowned boy, watching from the reeds.

There they go-a-playing off on the brown
sands, my darling boys.
O so merrily along, along!
Along and away, singing songs of saturday;
fetching nettle wine from places unseen;
taking other boys home into their dreams.

II

The sweetest of them all cannot help
but sing their dreams into lullabies.
storing desire itself in tin-can microphones,
stripped from the carriages of crippled taxi-men
who are listening like perverts for their crying wives.
O Netley! Marvin Road and the ghost of the lads club
haunt the checkouts. all flesh is crass. October
rolls around again, cackling like a cruel joke.
The drowned boy stares down and away from us.

My boys would enjoy themselves if not
for saying their endless goodbyes.
goodbye to this land of breakfasts that
set in. Goodbye, goodbye again.
The drowned boy plays again, making
fun in murky shallows, dragging fingers

over toes to hear us slip and swim and
scream.

Our faces only grow whiter, the softest
shallows pulling colour and washing pallid
over our eyelids. Swallowed up like bottom
feeding things. Held in place by broken tree
branch bones.

Space Force

They would not tell us.
Would not. Would not
Would not do.

       Where in the belt do they recreate the sun king?
    While forces go above to walk the skies and the firmament?
       With hands in hands and hands on six shooters?

Come with me now, Space Cowboy, saddle up into the horizon.
Ride over frontiersmen choking in the black emptiness and
turning to breathless ice and matter.
all that matters. And all that does not
Simply is.

Join me on the surface, kicking tin and diamonds from rainfall
and ground
But not earth.
Take your cosmic steed to the back of the place, and fill your
bag with moondust.

Ain't no lawman around here.
So rub the grey sand shards into your eyes, bring in the red
dawn which never sleeps.
Yee-haw!
Bring out your dead for the bug hunt baby;
Rest that Clanger's jaw on the saloon steps
      and bring that boot down!

bird eye

feeling at home,
a place by the sea,
making friends of
barnacle-picking washer-women
and talking of things I've never
known. I have never wanted to
smell the harbour; or cry the
storm through, pulling barnacles
from a soft hand. They've dragged
me in. all pies and cobble and
sloping doors. I have hated them
forever, using each other as bait,
covering themselves in guts and
bubbling at the moon.
still, the sun rises.

The Octopus

What did they see or
whom, on Providence edge?
where waters ebb and
black pools of mud all
crab-like ooze toward a doorstep
to murmur beside your letterbox.

necrotic giggling, nymphs of the
deep abound around even the
most gentle seaside town. a
greyness in the sky that drags
colour from the bone. a song in
deafening flow is the gentle roar of
the monsoon in the back of the throat.

the laughing boys sing down
at the cove, in rapturous dreams
of the women and the old,
pulling crab lines for one another,
bloodying stones for fun.
murmuring things of the deep,
below despair and roaring. a
red eye formed of foam.

the cove-beach boys play until
their fingers shake, where vertebrae
and waves will break and drag their
limpid digits home with clinging crabs
still spitting foam to find the beating
skins all quiet
and when crawling chaos vexes
to sweating dream, the stirring, swirling
vortices of steam, they beckon forth
the octopus from the spaces in between.

Labradors of the Unreal

We are leaving behind ourselves
in ways that don't seem to bother us.
When ourselves weren't things we were
all that acquainted with.

I'm left behind on the beach, where
dirt meets the licking sea-puppies of
water-rhythm and all of the words fall
off of the things.
all left are children, sand, spades
and buckets filled with small crabs.

All left are the black and white
thoughts of Bens and Grahams;
unreal memories of unreal children
playing unreal football on unreal cobbles.
unreal jumpers for real goalposts.
unreal books on unreal labradors by unreal authors.
an unreal past on an unreal seven p.m.

Welch in the bookshelf

candles passing backwards into veined hands
and stained rings that kiss candles before they burn.
a cross bound grandmother dripping blood to tempt the dawn
that, by now will always keep coming,
our robes don't fit us right,
and we embarrass the grandmother
we drop our shoeboxes and first shoes and your baby brother.
they had him bronzed and he sits on the mantle under the
cross-bound grandmother.

paces over faces
that rubbed coal on graves to hang on fridges
again rubbed coal and bark into paper.
your death embraces you and you greet it with a pencil.
cruel to be forced to play with dirt.
so sweet to be allowed to toy with dirt.

leaving time and present; left behind at grandfather's house
wrapping mud and silt over my bicycle wheels and onto my
legs.
pebbles into walls where i can imagine teeth cracking in two.
by the wall i stop
pausing to hear the boy whipping himself in the mausoleum
and think only of the cross-bound grandmother.
I return excitedly to my grandfather's house.

untitled

the thing breathing itself out of nilotic
mud, a cancerous aberration
of englishman's spirit. tawny owl

rain down rain down! rain so glee and
glib. porous as the stone they birthed
you on. soaking every drop to its core.

where the afterbirth of sunlight hurts
them twice the second time round,
barbarous tales of flesh rippled in your veins,

scheherazade in a maid's outfit,
behind walls to tell stories each night. veils
over stars, blackened sunshine. the ghosts of

christmas passed. there's no end in sight,
a plainfield geiner, a joke on the nightly.
news. this is not the world. this is not

america. this is not amniotic fluid
living in pond water. this is yeats
breathing his last whilst the dead child

waits under earth to be made new in
flesh. this is not death. this is no crypt.
a shudder in the loins engenders there.

asleep

I fell asleep again,
like a machine, aching
in its own skin.

lulled into a world
of dream skyscrapers
and clouds of life .
the city doesn't sleep
but it dreams.

bacall

the ghost of bette davis still claws at
       my tablecloth. watching my clock turn back
            a feeling of disease
             in the stomach
             of the home.

boiling bogart's blackened lung on the hearth
        albert brooks or another name
                   forms laughs of sounds
                       strung
                   to-get-her.
a.d. bennepaker watches

             tears
             fall
             beside
             the chrysler building.

       sincerity in the age of monterey.
     collision in the mechanics of desire.
     a misunderstanding of the oxygen
        in between the dust.

Diamond Doggerel

keep the aphid lysistrata flying.
I don't know, i didn't read it.
I was left alone at the station with
someone else's coat and a bindle of
my father's teeth. I was expected to
exchange them in kind with
Rudyard Kipling at some station further
along my travels.
not moving at all but travelling
an endless river
confusing memory and place
watching the rhino die
High noon in burma.
or is it spain? Franco
and a frail handshake sold to a dying
watch. I fled the old world, in cuba
i was a landed man. those boys were
mine! i came over here in a bindle in
nineteen ninety-one. khrushchev
commemorated my passage with
the end of history. it was at this exact
same time that i appeared in flesh
at the tate and vomited blood in
the rothko room or was it?
i again traced my essence
into the lines of a swedish crone
who would hassle the tobacconists
daughter and project dancing skeletons
onto full moons.what makes the grass
grow? blood blood blood. Alhazred or
Muad'Dib? I will forget it all. mislearned
cultures through conduits of soft
white bodies at typewriters. false ideas

as false memory. maybe a prophet came
maybe he was mad. All things must pass;
all great art beaten down; maybe this was
the crazy world of arthur brown? At the
W.I. they elect the leader of the thule
society, waiting for a bubbling in the chamber.
an echoing of eternity's waiting.
"a scream and then a sigh"; "I am not a
witch! god knows my name."; "out of college,
money's spent, see no future, pay no rent."
slouched and raving like diamond doggerel.
endless webs of culture.
i forget where i started.

War Poems
(for many different types of men)

1. for Marvin Gaye

We will all be shot by our fathers.
When vision becomes movement outside
of your thoughts;
Yes, you too, I suppose
Will be shot by your father.

2. for Lars Von Trier

I've played with dogs on holidays,
spent seven years with their remains.
I've spent an ice age dreaming of the
secret logic of burning trains.

Made dancers out of the dark,
forged beauty in a kiln.
Brought the last gasp of woman &
hate onto sixteen-millimeter film.

3. for Philip Mountbatten

alabaster sunrise,
rice paper skin moves
once more. a rippling
of veins, washing bile
over blackened teeth.

they've remade burma
in his image, reassembled
the viscount from the mire,
unwinding a force of riches
and sweat and mud.

the elephant: bare boned
and crying to be re-dead
carries the giggling skeleton
and his golden bough

and crown of spices
over the cinnamon sunset;
with corpse eyes all-a-twinkle
and arms billowing like willows

Into Bolivian Sky
(for Allen Ginsberg)

La paz! How real!?
Central line of dogged heat
to wind/ drum/ kite/ surf to
Bring back an African summer
When in Morocco
        shaking
I am swallowed up by the ass of the old man.
I am shaken by the swallowing of the boy.

Go→go→go→
To anywhere here, where
poverty/ sin/ even the feminine
Wants to wash my feet
Grey on white on face
On bowler hat- headedness.
I am dogged on this ship.
Drag a plantation family home and cast me into
        concrete; this citrus exploding.
Again into asphalt here
And again here/ to be/ spirituality/
For the darlings and birds along the isle of dogs.

Thinking again, I am leaving→ →
        followed by beards.
Men of beauty, beards of youth passing by them,
And into you.
Beyond a stream
And thru 2 me
Where new age men in dungaree,
        who see

airplane hashish jewish jesus
        where he
doesn't want to be.

I was lost watching.

When the bearded bum in buddha- dress sweats into nothing
and evaporates into bolivian sky.

Porcupine

I rearranged the lines at the zoo.
I put the dogs next to the lemurs and opened up the roof of
the aviary,
Then I kicked the sides and watched macaws and herons and
the albatross and the tawny owl ghosts choke the light out of
the sky and rain their plumage on my head.

I'd like to kiss the lines of people at the zoo.
The tigers and I would love to touch their faces and bottleneck
them around the aquarium with its dark lamps and large crabs
and lines and lines and lines.

I like to follow a way to the ends of the lines,
where no one is waiting.
and I can see the porcupine.
He sits in the sun and plays games with the flies;
His smile so demure, under his prickly disguise,
I sit down beside him and I gaze so sweetly
at my porcupine friend who is waking to meet me.

he's grown quite weary;
has never said a word.
for such a talkative zoo
that's just rather absurd.
still we'll sit all day
we'll move less and less.
until the zoo closes
and it's time for him to rest.
when dusk bleaches the sun
when he closes his eyes
moves away to his home;
says his silent goodbyes.

I'll see the porcupine soon at the end of line.
where it's just me and him
in the quiet part
of a talkative zoo
where I'll climb over the fence
and old friends become new.
In the evenings I like to climb into the trees and hold hands
with the chimps.
Things are much more simple here.

ACKNOWLEDGEMENTS

As with anything I ever begin writing it is always an absolute miracle when I finish the thing. As such, I would like to thank my fiancé Caroline for her constant love and enduring support; my mum, dad, and brother Sam for always being there, for better or worse; and Matt Hawes and Samuel Groves for being much more wonderful and interesting as friends and people than I could ever try to be, and making me all the better for it. At the same time but not at all this is dedicated to David Bowie. I would also be remiss not to thank the wonderful Paul Handley and all the folks at Bearded Badger for their support and patience, such a genuine and earnest champion of local writing is hardly found, and Paul's mission at Bearded Badger is something to be admired. It has been nothing but a pleasure to work with them.

TRA[verse]

For more information about the range of poetry on the TRA[verse] imprint, please visit:

www.beardedbadgerpublishing.com

or follow us on social media:

Facebook - **Bearded Badger Publishing**

Twitter - **@beardedbadgerpc**

Instagram - **@bearded_badger_publishing**